SH*T TRUMP SAYS

The Most **Terrific,** Very **Beautiful,** and
Tremendous Tweets and **Quotes** from our

—— **45TH PRESIDENT** ——

© 2017 Castle Point Publishing
All rights reserved. No portion of this book
may be reproduced or transmitted in any form
or by any means, electronic or mechanical,
including photocopying, recording, and other
information storage and retrieval systems,
without prior written permission of the publisher.

Castle Point Publishing
www.castlepointpub.com

ISBN: 978-0-9982297-1-3
Printed and bound in the United States of America
10 9 8 7 6 5 4

CONTENTS

I am the world's greatest person

Phone conversation with Australian
Prime Minister Malcolm Turnbull,
January 27, 2017

LOSERS!

Sorry losers and haters,
but my I.Q. is one of the
highest—and you all know it!
Please don't feel so stupid or
insecure, it's not your fault.

Twitter post, May 8, 2013

I am the BEST builder, just look at what I've built. Hillary can't build. Republican candidates can't build. They don't have a clue!

Twitter post, May 13, 2015

"In politics, and in life, ignorance is not a virtue." This is a primary reason that President Obama is the worst president in U.S. history!

Twitter post, May 16, 2016

How stupid are the people of Iowa?

Campaign speech in Fort Dodge, Iowa,
November 12, 2015

Happy Thanksgiving to all -- even the haters and losers!

Twitter post, November 27, 2013

Mitt Romney, who was one of the dumbest and worst candidates in the history of Republican politics, is now pushing me on tax returns. Dope!

Twitter post, February 25, 2016

Going to Ohio, home of one of the worst presidential candidates in history--Kasich. Can't debate, loves #ObamaCare--dummy!

Twitter post, November 23, 2015

**WORST GRAPHICS
AND STAGE BACKDROP
EVER AT THE OSCARS.
SHOW IS TERRIBLE,
REALLY BORING!**

Twitter post, February 22, 2015

I LOVE THE POORLY EDUCATED.

Caucus victory speech in Las Vegas, Nevada,
February 23, 2016

Remember this, the worst doctors (by far) are celebrity doctors. If you see their names, or read about them in the newspapers, stay away!

Twitter post, August 31, 2014

YES, ARNOLD SCHWARZENEGGER
DID A REALLY BAD JOB AS GOVERNOR
OF CALIFORNIA AND EVEN WORSE
ON THE APPRENTICE...BUT AT LEAST
HE TRIED HARD!

Twitter post, February 3, 2017

A guy walked into my office two weeks ago. He shook my hand, hugged me, sat down and said, "I have the worst flu I've ever had." **The guy looked like he was dying, and he'd just shaken my hand. I said, "Why did you shake my hand?" People don't have a clue. It's disgusting.**

Interview with *Playboy* magazine, 2004

It makes me feel
so good to hit
"sleazebags" back --
much better than
seeing a psychiatrist
(which I never have!)

Twitter post, November 19, 2012

Amazing how the haters & losers keep tweeting the name "F**kface Von Clownstick" like they are so original & like no one else is doing it...

Twitter post, May 3, 2013

[IN RESPONSE TO PROTESTERS:]

IF YOU SEE SOMEBODY GETTING READY TO THROW A TOMATO, KNOCK THE CRAP OUT OF 'EM, WOULD YOU?

Rally speech in Iowa, February 1, 2016

You can only smile
when the losers of
the world try so
hard to put down
successful people.
Just remember, they
all want to be YOU!

Twitter post, December 3, 2013

EVERY TIME I SPEAK OF THE HATERS AND LOSERS I DO SO WITH GREAT LOVE AND AFFECTION. **THEY CANNOT HELP THE FACT THAT THEY WERE BORN FUCKED UP!**

Twitter post, September 28, 2014

WINNING

I was always the **best** athlete. . . . I was always the **best** at sports.

Interview with author Michael D'Antonio, 2014

PART OF THE BEAUTY OF ME IS THAT I'M VERY RICH.

Interview with *Good Morning America*,
March 17, 2011

BEAUTIFUL, FAMOUS, SUCCESSFUL, MARRIED— I'VE HAD THEM ALL, SECRETLY, THE WORLD'S BIGGEST NAMES, BUT UNLIKE GERALDO [RIVERA] I DON'T TALK ABOUT IT.

In *Think Big and Kick Ass in Business and Life*,
published in 2007

Many people have said
I'm the world's greatest writer
of 140 character sentences.

Twitter post, July 21, 2014

Actresses just call to see if they can go out with him and things.

Speaking about himself in the
persona of John Miller, a supposed
spokesman for Donald Trump, 1991

Many people have
commented that my
fragrance "Success"
is the best scent &
lasts the longest.

Twitter post, July 21, 2014

I AM IN LAS VEGAS,

AT THE BEST HOTEL [BY FAR],

TRUMP INTERNATIONAL.

Twitter post, February 22, 2016

I have over seven million hits on social media re Crooked Hillary Clinton.

Twitter post, July 6, 2016

Happy New Year to all, **including to my many enemies and those who have fought me and lost so badly they just don't know what to do.** Love!

Twitter post, December 31, 2016

@Helena_Torry

I consider myself too perfect and have no faults.

Twitter post, January 13, 2014

Romney campaign used me in 6 primary states and won every one- they should have used me in Florida and Ohio & he would be President.

Twitter post, November 8, 2012

It has not been easy for me, it has not been easy for me. And you know I started off in Brooklyn, my father gave me a small loan of a million dollars.

Comment at NBC-sponsored town hall,
October 26, 2015

The show is "Trump" and it is sold-out performances everywhere.

Interview with *Playboy* magazine, 1990

Certainly a businessperson on television has never had anything close to this success. It's like being a rock star. Six people do nothing but sort my mail.

Interview with *Playboy* magazine, 2004

BLACK ENTERTAINERS LOVE DONALD TRUMP.

RUSSELL SIMMONS TOLD ME THAT.

Interview with *Playboy* magazine, 2004

Show me someone
without an ego, and
I'll show you a loser -
having a healthy ego,
or high opinion of yourself,
is a real positive in life!

Facebook post, December 9, 2013

Some people have an ability to negotiate. It's an art you're basically born with. You either have it or you don't.

Interview with the *The Washington Post*,
November 15, 1984

It would take an hour-and-a-half to learn everything there is to learn about missiles. . . . I think I know most of it anyway.

Interview with the *The Washington Post*,
November 15, 1984

Some people have
a talent for golf.
I just happen to
have a talent
for making money.

Interview with *Playboy* magazine, 2004

I build the best buildings, and I'm the biggest developer in New York by far.

Interview with *The New York Times*,
September 25, 1999

I DO WHINE because I want to win and I'm not happy about not winning and **I AM A WHINER** and **I KEEP WHINING** and **WHINING** until I win.

Interview with CNN's Chris Cuomo,
August 11, 2015

My attitude is if
somebody's willing
to pay me $225,000
to make a speech,
it seems stupid not
to show up.

Interview with *The New Yorker*,
May 19, 1997

SOME PEOPLE AREN'T MEANT TO BE RICH. . . . IT'S JUST SOMETHING YOU HAVE, SOMETHING YOU'RE BORN WITH.

Interview with *Playboy* magazine, 2004

I've never used an ATM.
Of course, I always have
access to money,
and I have hundreds
of checking accounts.

Interview with *Playboy* magazine, 2004

I COULD stand
in the middle of
Fifth Avenue and
SHOOT
SOMEBODY
and I
WOULDN'T LOSE
ANY VOTERS.

Rally speech in Sioux Center, Iowa,
January 23, 2016

I would like to promise
and pledge to all of my voters
and supporters and to all of
the people of the United States
that **I will totally accept the
results** of this great and
historic presidential election.

IF I WIN.

Presidential debate in Las Vegas, Nevada,
October 19, 2016

I will be the greatest jobs president that God ever created. I tell you that.

Campaign launch speech, June 16, 2015

I'm the king of debt.
I understand debt
better than probably
anybody. I know how
to deal with debt
very well. I love debt.

Appearance on CNN, May 9, 2016

And just thinking to myself right now,
we should just cancel the election
and just give it to Trump, right?
What are we even having it for?
What are we having it for?

Rally speech in Toledo, Ohio, October 27, 2016

NOBODY
HAS MORE
RESPECT
FOR WOMEN.
NOBODY!

[To French President Emmanuel Macron
and his wife, Brigitte Macron:]

You're in such GOOD SHAPE. She's in such **GOOD PHYSICAL SHAPE.** Beautiful.

Official visit to France, July 13, 2017

I don't even wait.

And when you're a star,
they let you do it.
You can do anything. . . .

GRAB 'EM BY THE PUSSY.

Off-the-air recorded conversation
with Billy Bush, 2005

I moved on her like a bitch.

But I couldn't get there.
And she was married.

Off-the-air recorded conversation
with Billy Bush, 2005

This was locker room banter, a private conversation that took place many years ago. Bill Clinton has said far worse to me on the golf course—not even close. I apologize if anyone was offended.

Statement in the aftermath of leaked conversation with Billy Bush, October 7, 2016

I think the ONLY DIFFERENCE BETWEEN ME AND THE OTHER CANDIDATES is that I'm more honest and MY WOMEN ARE MORE BEAUTIFUL.

Interview with *The New York Times*,
November 17, 1999

26,000 unreported sexual assaults in the military-only 238 convictions. What did these geniuses expect when they put men & women together?

Twitter post, May 7, 2013

Did Crooked Hillary
help disgusting
[check out sex tape
and past] Alicia M
become a U.S. citizen
so she could use her
in the debate?

Twitter post, September 30, 2016

@ariannahuff

IS UNATTRACTIVE

BOTH INSIDE AND OUT.

I FULLY UNDERSTAND

WHY HER FORMER

HUSBAND LEFT HER

FOR A MAN- HE MADE

A GOOD DECISION.

Twitter post, August 28, 2012

Amazing that Crooked Hillary can do a hit ad on me concerning women when her husband was the WORST abuser of woman in U.S. political history!

Twitter post, May 17, 2016

[ON RUNNING FOR PRESIDENT DESPITE
HIS HISTORY WITH WOMEN:]

Can you imagine how
controversial I'd be?
You think about [Bill Clinton]
with the women. How about
me with the women?

Can you imagine?

Interview with CNBC's Chris Mattews, 1998

[ON BILL CLINTON'S SEXUAL ASSAULT ACCUSERS:]

The whole group, it's truly an unattractive cast of characters— Linda Tripp, Lucianne Goldberg— I mean, this woman—I watch her on television, just vomiting. She is so bad. The whole group— Paula Jones, Lewinsky—it's just a really unattractive group.

Appearance on Fox News, 1998

IT DOESN'T REALLY MATTER WHAT [THE MEDIA] WRITE AS LONG AS YOU'VE GOT A YOUNG AND BEAUTIFUL PIECE OF A**.

Interview with *Esquire* magazine, 1991

While @BetteMidler is an
extremely unattractive woman,
I refuse to say that because I always
insist on being politically correct.

Twitter post, October 28, 2012

A person who's
FLAT-CHESTED
is very hard
to be a 10, OK?

Interview with Howard Stern, September 2005

"@ForeverMcIn: @realDonaldTrump how much would it take for you to make out with Rosie O'Donnell?" One trillion, at least!

Twitter post, March 1, 2013

IF I WERE RUNNING "THE VIEW,"
I'D FIRE ROSIE [O'DONNELL].
I mean, I'd look her right in that
FAT, UGLY FACE OF HERS,
I'd say, "Rosie, you're fired."

Interview with *Entertainment Tonight*, 2006

[ON CALLING FOX NEWS HOST MEGYN KELLY A BIMBO:]

OVER YOUR LIFE, MEGYN, YOU'VE BEEN CALLED A LOT WORSE. ISN'T THAT RIGHT? WOULDN'T YOU SAY?

Interview with Fox News's Megyn Kelly, May 17, 2016

I know politicians who love women who don't even want to be known for that— because they might lose the gay vote.

Interview with *Playboy* magazine, 1990

I'VE NEVER BEEN
THE KIND OF GUY
WHO TAKES HIS SON
OUT TO CENTRAL
PARK TO PLAY CATCH,
BUT I THINK I'M A
GOOD FATHER.

Interview with *Playboy* magazine, 2004

I like kids. I mean,

I won't do anything to take care of them.

I'll supply funds,

and she'll take care of the kids.

Interview with Howard Stern, 2005

[ON WOMEN WHO HAVE ABORTIONS:]

THERE HAS TO BE SOME FORM OF PUNISHMENT.

Interview with Chris Matthews during town hall meeting in Green Bay, Wisconsin, March 30, 2016

She does have a very nice figure. I'VE SAID THAT IF IVANKA WEREN'T MY DAUGHTER, PERHAPS I'D BE DATING HER.

Interview with ABC's *The View*, 2006

[IN REFERENCE TO HILLARY CLINTON:]

Such a NASTY woman.

Live presidential debate, October 19, 2016

If I told the real stories of my experiences with women, often seemingly very happily married and important women, this book would be a guaranteed best-seller.

In *Trump: The Art of the Comeback*, 1997

For a man to be successful he needs support at home, just like my father had from my mother, not someone who is always griping and bitching.

In *Trump: The Art of the Comeback*, 1997

FAKE
NEWS!

THIS VERY EXPENSIVE GLOBAL WARMING BULLSHIT HAS GOT TO STOP. OUR PLANET IS FREEZING, RECORD LOW TEMPS, AND OUR GW SCIENTISTS ARE STUCK IN ICE.

Twitter post, January 1, 2014

It's freezing and snowing in New York--we need global warming!

Twitter post, November 7, 2012

I have been drawing **very big** and enthusiastic crowds, but the media refuses to show or discuss them. Something **very big** is happening!

Twitter post, August 21, 2016

The failing @nytimes is truly one of the worst newspapers. They knowingly write lies and never even call to fact check. Really bad people!

Twitter post, March 13, 2016

It is being reported
by virtually everyone,
and is a fact,
that the media pile
on against me
is the worst in American
political history!

Twitter post, August 23, 2016

Any negative polls
are fake news,
just like the
CNN, ABC, NBC
polls in the election.
Sorry, people want
border security and
extreme vetting.

Twitter post, February 6, 2017

As a very active
President with lots
of things happening,
it is not possible for
my surrogates to stand
at podium with
perfect accuracy!

Twitter post, May 12, 2017

I THINK THE THING I'M WORST AT IS MANAGING THE PRESS.

Interview with *The New Yorker*, May 19, 1997

Do you mind if I sit back a little? Because your breath is very bad—it really is.

Interview with Larry King, April 15, 1989

*IT IS MY OPINION THAT
MANY OF THE LEAKS COMING
OUT OF THE WHITE HOUSE
ARE FABRICATED LIES MADE
UP BY THE #FAKENEWS MEDIA.*

Twitter post, May 28, 2017

RUSSIAN OFFICIALS
MUST BE LAUGHING AT THE U.S. & HOW A LAME EXCUSE FOR WHY THE DEMS LOST THE ELECTION HAS TAKEN OVER THE FAKE NEWS.

Twitter post, May 30, 2017

The Fake News Media works hard at disparaging & demeaning my use of social media because they don't want America to hear the real story!

Twitter post, May 28, 2017

I HAVE RAISED/GIVEN A TREMENDOUS AMOUNT OF MONEY TO OUR GREAT VETERANS, AND HAVE GOT NOTHING BUT BAD PUBLICITY FOR DOING SO. WATCH!

Twitter post, May 31, 2016

My twitter has become so powerful that I can actually make my enemies tell the truth.

Twitter post, October 17, 2012

Hard to believe that with 24/7 #Fake News on CNN, ABC, NBC, CBS, NYTIMES & WAPO, the Trump base is getting stronger!

Twitter post, August 7, 2017

MIRROR, MIRROR

@cher--I don't wear a
"rug"—it's mine.
And I promise not
to talk about your
massive plastic surgeries
that didn't work.

Twitter post, November 13, 2012

IF A LIMO PULLS UP IN FRONT OF TRUMP TOWER, HUNDREDS OF PEOPLE GATHER AROUND, EVEN IF IT'S NOT MINE.

Interview with *Playboy* magazine, 2004

You think I'm going to change?

I'M NOT CHANGING.

Press conference, May 31, 2016

I will never change
this hairstyle, I like it.
It fits my head.
**Those who criticize
me are only losers**
and envy people.

Interview with *Veja* magazine, 2014

I get up, take a shower and wash my hair. . . . Once I have it the way I like it—even though nobody else likes it— I spray it and it's good for the day.

Interview with *Playboy* magazine, 2004

Wait a minute—so if I take hair spray and I spray it in my apartment, which is all sealed, you're telling me that affects the ozone layer? "Yes?" I say no way folks. No way.

Campaign speech in Charleston, West Virginia,
May 5, 2016

*I like [money],
but I don't need it.
I like it and I feel
I should have it
and I think it would
be inappropriate for
me not to have it. . . .
I don't do it because
I need it. I do it for
other reasons.*

Interview with *The Washington Post*,
November 15, 1984

[ON KENTUCKY SENATOR RAND PAUL:]

I never attacked him on his look, and believe me, there's plenty of subject matter right there.

Presidential debate, September 16, 2015

[WHEN ASKED ABOUT HIS FOREIGN POLICY CONSULTANTS:]

I'm speaking with myself, number one, because I have a VERY GOOD BRAIN and I've said a lot of things.

Interview with MSNBC's *Morning Joe*, March 16, 2016

I actually have low blood pressure. . . . **The doctor said, "Man you have the blood pressure of a great, great athlete who is 20 years old."**

Campaign speech, Waterbury, Connecticut,
April 23, 2016

My fingers are long and beautiful,

as, it has been well documented,

are various other parts of my body.

Interview with *Page Six*, 2011

The cheap 12 inch sq. marble tiles behind speaker at UN always bothered me. I will replace with beautiful large marble slabs if they ask me.

Twitter post, October 3, 2012

I FEEL LIKE A SUPERMODEL EXCEPT, LIKE, TIMES 10, OK? IT'S TRUE. I'M A SUPERMODEL.

Campaign speech in Arizona, June 18, 2016

DRAIN THE SWAMP AND BUILD A YUGE WALL

Happy Cinco de Mayo!
The best taco bowls are
made in Trump Tower Grill.
I love Hispanics!

Twitter post, May 5, 2016

When Mexico sends its people, they're not sending their best. . . . They're bringing drugs. They're bringing crime. They're rapists.

Candidacy announcement speech, June 16, 2015

I will build a great, great wall on our southern border, and I will have Mexico pay for that wall.

Candidacy announcement speech,
June 16, 2015

*From an economic issue,
[the border wall] is
the least important thing
we were talking about.*

Phone call with Mexican president
Enrique Pena Nieto, January 27, 2017

I have brought millions
of people into the
Republican Party,
while the Dems
are going down.
Establishment wants
to kill this movement!

Twitter post, March 3, 2016

*And we won't be using
a man like Secretary Kerry . . .
[who] goes into a bicycle race
at 72 years old, and falls
and breaks his leg.
I won't be doing that.*

Candidacy announcement speech, June 16, 2015

[ON JOHN MCCAIN:]

HE'S NOT A WAR HERO.

HE'S A WAR HERO BECAUSE HE WAS CAPTURED.

I LIKE PEOPLE THAT WEREN'T CAPTURED.

Speech in Ames, Iowa, July 18, 2015

Cryin' Chuck Schumer stated recently, "I do not have confidence in him (James Comey) any longer." Then acts so indignant. #draintheswamp

Twitter post, May 9, 2017

The reason I am staying
in Bedminster, N.J.,
a beautiful community,
is that staying in NYC is
much more expensive
and disruptive. Meetings!

Twitter post, May 6, 2017

Watched protests yesterday but was under the impression that we just had an election! Why didn't these people vote? **Celebs hurt cause badly.**

Twitter post, January 22, 2017

GETTING READY FOR
MY BIG FOREIGN TRIP.
WILL BE STRONGLY
PROTECTING
AMERICAN INTERESTS -
THAT'S WHAT
I LIKE TO DO!

Twitter post, May 19, 2017

SOMEONE SHOULD
LOOK INTO WHO PAID FOR
THE SMALL ORGANIZED
RALLIES YESTERDAY.
THE ELECTION IS OVER!

Twitter post, April 16, 2017

I am being investigated for firing the FBI Director by the man who told me to fire the FBI Director! Witch Hunt

Twitter post, June 16, 2017

WE CAN'T CONTINUE TO ALLOW CHINA TO RAPE OUR COUNTRY, AND THAT'S WHAT THEY'RE DOING.

Campaign speech in Fort Wayne, Indiana,
May 1, 2016

Do you think **Putin** will be going to The Miss Universe Pageant in November in Moscow - if so, **will he become my new best friend?**

Twitter post, June 18, 2013

Someone incorrectly stated that the phrase "DRAIN THE SWAMP" was no longer being used by me. Actually, we will always be trying to DTS.

Twitter post, December 22, 2016

I know more about ISIS than the generals do. Believe me.

Campaign speech in Fort Dodge, Iowa, November 12, 2015

LOCK YOUR DOORS,
folks, OK?
LOCK YOUR DOORS.
No, it's a big problem. . . .
We have our **INCOMPETENT
GOVERNMENT** people letting
them in by the thousands,
and who knows,
WHO KNOWS,
maybe it's **ISIS.**

Campaign speech in Warwick, Rhode Island,
April 25, 2016

*[Barack Obama]
is the founder of ISIS.
He's the founder of
ISIS,
OK?
He's the founder.
He founded ISIS
and I would say
the co-founder
would be
crooked
Hillary Clinton.*

Campaign speech in Sunrise, Florida,
August 10, 2016

Look at my African-American over here! Look at him! Are you the greatest?

Campaign speech in Redding, California,
June 6, 2016

By the way, if
[Hillary Clinton]
gets to pick her judges,
nothing you can do, folks.

**Although the
Second Amendment
people—maybe there
is, I don't know.**

Campaign speech in Wilmington,
North Carolina, August 9, 2016

Crooked Hillary has **ZERO leadership ability**. As Bernie Sanders says, she has **bad judgement**. Constantly **playing the women's card** - it is sad!

Twitter post, May 6, 2016

GREAT MOVE ON DELAY [BY V. PUTIN] - I ALWAYS KNEW HE WAS VERY SMART!

Twitter post, December 30, 2016

Why is Obama playing basketball today? That is why our country is in trouble!

Twitter post, November 6, 2012

We will immediately repeal and replace ObamaCare - and nobody can do that like me. We will save $'s and have much better healthcare!

Twitter post, February 9, 2016

I'm just a f------ businessman.

Interview with *Fortune* magazine, April 19, 2004

Good people don't go into government.

Interview with *The Advocate*,
February 2000

IT'S TRUE,
IT'S IMPORTANT,
AND SPELLING
DOESN'T COUNT

[*The New York Times*]
don't write good.

Interview with Fox News' *Hannity*, August 1, 2016

DESPITE THE CONSTANT NEGATIVE PRESS

COVFEFE

Twitter post, May 31, 2017

I won the popular
vote if you deduct
the millions of people
who voted illegally

Twitter post, November 27, 2016

I WAS DOWN THERE,

AND I WATCHED OUR POLICE

AND OUR FIREMEN,

DOWN ON 7-ELEVEN,

DOWN AT THE WORLD TRADE CENTER,

RIGHT AFTER IT CAME DOWN.

Campaign speech in Buffalo,
New York, April 18, 2016

LEIGHTWEIGHT CHOCKER MARCO RUBIO LOOKS LIKE A LITTLE BOY ON STAGE. NOT PRESIDENTIAL MATERIAL!

Twitter post, February 26, 2016

Wow, every poll said I
won the debate last night.

Great honer!

Twitter post, February 26, 2016

Ted Cruz is totally unelectable, if he even gets to run [born in Canada]. Will loose big to Hillary.

Twitter post, January 31, 2016

An 'extremely credible source' has called my office and told me that Obama's birth certificate is a fraud.

Twitter post, August 6, 2012

The concept of global warming was created by and for the Chinese in order to make U.S. manufacturing non-competitive.

Twitter post, November 6, 2012

Hillary Clinton should not be given national security briefings in that **she is a lose cannon** with **extraordinarily bad judgement & insticts.**

Twitter post, July 29, 2016

His grandmother in Kenya said, "Oh no, he was born in Kenya and I was there and I witnessed the birth."

Interview with MSNBC's *Morning Joe*,
April 7, 2011

You may get **AIDS** by kissing.

Interview with Howard Stern, 1993

They had no definitive
proof against Tom Brady
or #patriots. If Hillary
doesn't have to produce
Emails, why should Tom?
Very unfair!

Twitter post, May 11, 2015

Robert Pattinson should not take back Kristen Stewart. She cheated on him like a dog & will do it again--just watch. He can do much better!

Twitter post, October 17, 2012

.@katyperry is no bargain but I don't like John Mayer-- he dates and tells-- be careful Katy (just watch!).

Twitter post, October 19, 2012

@katyperry
Katy, what the hell were you thinking when you married loser Russell Brand. There is a guy who has got nothing going, a waste!

Twitter post, October 16, 2014

All the dress shops are sold out in Washington. It's hard to find a great dress for this inauguration.

Interview with *The New York Times*,
January 9, 2017

FLIP-FLOPS

I have no intention of running for president.

Interview with *Time* magazine, September 14, 1987

I am officially running for president.

Candidacy announcement speech, June 16, 2015

I don't want it for myself. I don't need it for myself.

Interview with ABC News,
November 20, 2015

I wanted to do this for myself. . . . I had to do it for myself.

Interview with *Time* magazine,
August 18, 2015

I'm not a POLITICIAN.

Interview with CNN, August 11, 2015

I'm no different than a POLITICIAN running for office.

Interview with *The New York Times*,
July 28, 2015

I'm totally pro-choice.

Interview with Fox News, October 31, 1999

I'm pro-life.

Speech at the Conservative Political Action
Conference, February 10, 2011

Look, I'm very pro-choice.

Interview with *Meet the Press*,
October 24, 1999

I am very, very proud to say that I'm pro-life.

Republican presidential debate,
Cleveland, Ohio, August 6, 2015

IF I EVER RAN FOR OFFICE, I'D DO BETTER AS A DEMOCRAT THAN AS A REPUBLICAN—AND THAT'S NOT BECAUSE I'D BE MORE LIBERAL, BECAUSE I'M CONSERVATIVE.

Interview with *Playboy* magazine, March 1990

I'M A REGISTERED REPUBLICAN. I'M A PRETTY CONSERVATIVE GUY. I'M SOMEWHAT LIBERAL ON SOCIAL ISSUES, ESPECIALLY HEALTH CARE, ETC.

Interview with Larry King, October 8, 1999

I've actually been an activist Democrat and Republican.

Interview with Larry King, October 8, 1999

I think the institution
of marriage should
be between a man
and a woman.

Interview with *The Advocate* magazine,
February 15, 2000

If two people dig each other, they dig each other.

Blog post on Trump University's Trump Blog,
December 22, 2005

I'm against gay marriage.

Interview with Fox News, April 14, 2011

It's always good to do things nice and complicated so that nobody can figure it out.

Comment published in *The New Yorker*,
May 19, 1997

The simplest approach is often the most effective.

In *Trump: The Art of the Deal*, 1987

My attention span is short.

In *Trump: Surviving at the Top*, 1990

I have an attention span that's as long as it has to be.

Interview with *Time* magazine,
August 18, 2015

I do listen to people.

I hire experts.

I hire top, top people.

And I do listen.

Republican presidential debate, Greenville,
South Carolina, February 13, 2016

My primary consultant is myself.

Interview with MSNBC's *Morning Joe*,
March 16, 2016

I surround myself
with good people,
and then I give
myself the luxury
of trusting them.

In *Trump: Surviving at the Top*, 1990

My motto is "Hire the best people, and don't trust them."

In *Trump: Think Big*, 2009

Stay as close
to home
as possible.
Travel is
time-consuming and,
in my opinion,
boring.

In *Trump: Surviving at the Top*, 1990

**There's no excuse
for staying home;
the world's
too fantastic
to miss out on it.
I wish I could
travel more.**

In *Trump: Think Like a
Billionaire*, 2004

If you can avoid an altercation, do so.

In *Trump: Think Like a Billionaire*, 2004

If someone attacks you, do not hesitate. Go for the jugular.

In *Trump: Think Big*, 2009

I think I've been a very good husband.

Interview with CNN, February 9, 2011

What the hell do I know, I've been divorced twice?

In *Trump: Think Big*, 2007

I KNOW HILLARY AND I THINK SHE'D MAKE A GREAT PRESIDENT.

Blog post on Trump University's
Trump Blog, March 13, 2008

HILLARY WILL BE A DISASTER AS A PRESIDENT.

Interview with NBC News,
July 9, 2015

I'm not a hunter
and don't approve
of killing animals.
I strongly disagree
with my sons who
are hunters.

Twitter post, March 15, 2012

My sons love to hunt. They are members of the NRA, very proudly. I am a big believer in the Second Amendment.

Speech in Ayrshire, Scotland, July 31, 2015

Millions and millions of women—
cervical cancer, breast cancer—
are helped by Planned Parenthood.
So you can say whatever you want,
but they have millions of women
going through Planned Parenthood
that are helped greatly.

Republican presidential debate in
Houston, Texas, February 25, 2016

But Planned Parenthood should absolutely be defunded. I mean, if you look at what's going on with that, it's terrible.

Interview with *Fox News*
Sunday, October 18, 2015

THE ELECTORAL COLLEGE IS A DISASTER FOR A DEMOCRACY.

Twitter post, November 6, 2012